Fatty Acid Metabolism
in Microorganisms

E. R. SQUIBB LECTURES ON

Presented at the Institute of Microbiology
Rutgers, the State University of New Jersey

F. M. Strong, *Topics in Microbial Chemistry,* **1956**

F. H. Stodola, *Chemical Transformations
by Microorganisms,* **1957**

V. H. Cheldelin, *Metabolic Pathways
in Microorganisms,* **1960**

K. Hofmann, *Fatty Acid Metabolism
in Microorganisms,* **1962**

Fatty Acid Metabolism in Microorganisms

By KLAUS HOFMANN
Professor of Biochemistry

University of Pittsburgh
School of Medicine

NEW YORK · LONDON, JOHN WILEY & SONS, INC.

In recognition of the importance of cooperation between chemist and microbiologist the E. R. Squibb Lectures on Chemistry of Microbial Products were established with the support of The Squibb Institute for Medical Research in 1955.   The lectures are presented annually in the fall at the Institute of Microbiology, Rutgers, the State University of New Jersey, New Brunswick, New Jersey.

PREFACE

The invitation to deliver the 1962 Squibb Lectures on Chemistry of Microbial Products was an honor which provided me with a welcome opportunity to summarize our studies dealing with some phases of fatty acid metabolism in microorganisms and to bring them into focus with recent developments. The experimental work has been carried out in the chemistry and biochemistry departments of the University of Pittsburgh since 1947. The book is divided into three chapters, which deal, respectively, with the discovery and chemistry of cyclopropane fatty acids, the chemical nature of monounsaturated fatty acids in bacteria, the quantitative estimation of fatty acids in bacterial lipids, the biosynthesis of the cyclopropane ring, and finally the anaerobic biosynthesis of monounsaturated fatty acids in microorganisms. The presentation is critical and influenced by the author's own point of view. No attempt is made to provide a comprehensive summary of the literature, and apologies are offered to investigators whose contributions have been omitted.

The experimental studies could not have been carried out without the devoted help of a number of former students and colleagues, and I wish to express my very sincere appreciation to Drs. Henis, Jucker, Liu, Lucas, Marco, Miller, O'Leary, Panos, Sax, Tausig, Yoho, Young, and the late Dr. Orochena for their untiring efforts. I also wish to express my thanks to Professors Axelrod and Jeffrey of the University of Pittsburgh for many helpful discussions.

This little book will fulfill its mission if it stimulates further inquiry into the neglected but intriguing field of microbial lipid metabolism.

K. HOFMANN

Pittsburgh, Pennsylvania
April, 1963

ACKNOWLEDGMENT

The author wishes to express his gratitude to *Biochemistry*, to the *Journal of the American Chemical Society*, to the *Journal of Biological Chemistry*, and to *Federation Proceedings* for their permission to reproduce certain figures and tables.

K. H.

CONTENTS

CHAPTER 1

LACTOBACILLIC ACID, A NOVEL MICROBIAL METABOLITE

1. DISCOVERY OF LACTOBACILLIC ACID

The observation (1–7) that unsaturated fatty acids exert a marked sparing action on the biotin requirements of certain lactic acid organisms prompted initiation of our systematic studies on the chemical nature of bacterial fatty acids. These studies, which led to the discovery of lactobacillic acid and to the recognition of *cis*-vaccenic acid as an important constituent of bacteria, provided the structural foundation for investigations of fatty acid metabolism in these lower forms of life.

The chemical nature of the fatty acids of *Lactobacillus arabinosus* (8, 9), *Lactobacillus casei* (10), *Agrobacterium (Phytomonas) tumefaciens* (11), and of a group C *Streptococcus* species (12) was determined in detail. The organisms were grown on essentially lipid-free media and fatty acids were isolated in the usual manner. Autoclaving with dilute acid must precede extraction, since some 80% of the fatty acids are present in the bacteria in a "bound" form not soluble in mixtures of acetone and ether. The lipids were

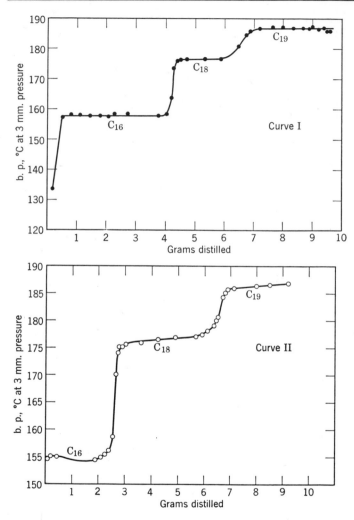

Fig. 1.1. Separation of methyl esters of fatty acids derived from *L. arabinosus* (curve I); *L. casei* (curve II); *Streptococcus hemolyticus,* group C (curve III); *Agrobacterium tumefaciens* (curve IV).

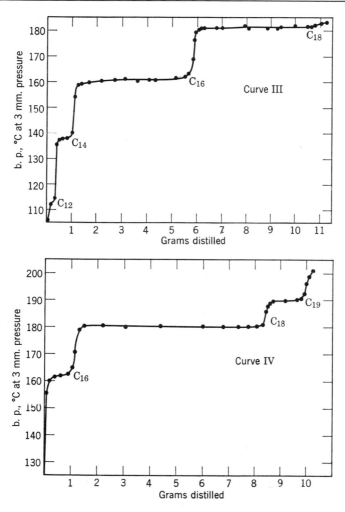

Fig. 1.1 *continued.*

saponified, the fatty acids converted into the methyl esters, and the ensuing ester mixture was separated into various components by fractional distillation. Inspection of typical distillation curves (Fig. 1.1), relating boiling point to amount distilled, shows the prominent presence of fatty acids containing 16 and 18 carbon atoms with lower fatty acids being present in small proportions. The presence of esters with boiling points above methyl stearate in the ester mixture derived from *L. arabinosus, L. casei,* and *A. tumefaciens* is of particular interest. Saponification of this highest boiling fraction gave a low melting (28–29°) crystalline acid of the composition $C_{19}H_{36}O_2$, which was given the name

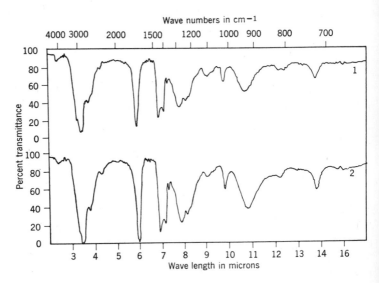

Fig. 1.2. Infrared absorption spectra of cyclopropane fatty acids. (1) "Phytomonic" acid from *A. tumefaciens.* (2) Lactobacillic acid from *L. casei.*

TABLE 1.1

Comparison of Main X-ray Spacings of Lactobacillic Acid from *L. arabinosus* and from *A. tumefaciens*

L. arabinosus	*A. tumefaciens*
Main Short Spacings	
4.65 M *	4.67 S †
4.35 M	4.38 M
4.07 M−	4.30 S
3.78 W ‡	4.07 W+
3.58 W+	3.81 W
3.42 W−	3.61 W
	3.43 W−
Long Spacing	
41.0	41.4

* M = medium
† S = strong
‡ W = weak

lactobacillic acid in view of its first isolation from a lactobacillus. Lactobacillic acid from *L. arabinosus* and *L. casei* is identical as concerns melting point, infrared absorption spectrum, and x-ray diffraction pattern. Lactobacillic acid is also identical with phytomonic acid (11), a compound previously isolated from *A. tumefaciens* whose true chemical nature had not been recognized by earlier investigators (13–17). The matching infrared absorption spectra (Fig. 1.2), x-ray diffraction patterns (Table 1.1), and melting points offer unequivocal evidence for identity. Lactobacillic acid appears to be a major constituent of the bacterial phospholipids (18).

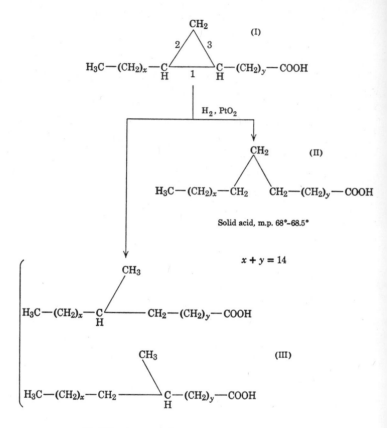

Fig. 1.3. Hydrogenolysis products of lactobacillic acid.

2. STRUCTURE OF LACTOBACILLIC ACID

The behavior of lactobacillic acid (8, 9) which provides the key to its chemical constitution is illustrated on Fig. 1.3. The acid is stable toward oxidizing agents but undergoes hydrogenolysis in presence of platinum and hydrogen with absorption of one mole of hydrogen. The resulting mixture of hydrogenation products contains nonadecanoic acid plus a product also containing 19 carbon atoms which melts at 13 to 14°, and on the basis of C-methyl determinations, possesses a branched carbon-chain. The latter material consists of a mixture of branched chain acids later recognized as DL-11- and DL-12-methyloctadecanoic acids. These materials arise from the simultaneous hydrogenolysis of the carbon-carbon bonds 2 and 3 in the lactobacillic acid molecule. Treatment with hydrogen bromide in glacial acetic acid converts lactobacillic acid into a mixture of mono-bromononadecanoic acids (see Chapter 2, section 4).

The chemical behavior of lactobacillic acid, i.e., its stability toward oxidation and its lability toward hydrogen bromide and hydrogenolysis, coupled with the fact that hydrogenolysis produces three acids—one of which contains a straight carbon chain (nonadecanoic acid)—pointed to the presence in lactobacillic acid of a cyclopropane ring. Stability toward oxidation and lability to hydrogenolysis and hydrogen bromide are characteristic properties of this particular ring system. The infrared absorption spectrum (Fig. 1.4, curve 1) supports the cyclopropane nature of lactobacillic acid. The spectrum exhibits the characteristic cyclopropane absorption maximum at 9.8 μ (19), which disappears on hydrogenation (curve 2).

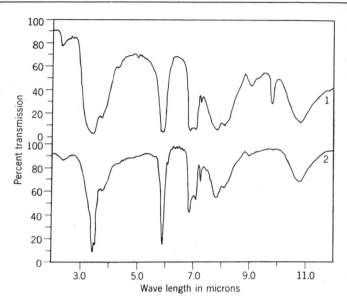

Fig. 1.4. Infrared absorption spectra of lactobacillic acid and one of its hydrogenation products. (1) Lactobacillic acid from *L. arabinosus*. (2) Liquid hydrogenation product.

All of the properties cited fit formula I (Fig. 1.3) as a likely structure for lactobacillic acid with the position of the cyclopropane ring unassigned.

3. LABORATORY SYNTHESIS OF LONG-CHAIN FATTY ACIDS CONTAINING THE CYCLOPROPANE RING

Although the position of the methylene bridge cannot be established by the reactions described in Chapter 1, section 2, structures for lactobacillic acid with the ring located in the 9,10 and 11,12 positions were considered likely because of their relation to the monoethenoid fatty acids (9-octadecenoic and 11-octadecenoic acids) which occur in bacterial lipids. If we consider the stereochemistry of this type of molecule, it is apparent that each position isomeric cyclopropane fatty acid can occur in four stereoisomeric forms, two of which belong to the *cis,* the other to the *trans* series. These forms are illustrated for the 9,10-compounds in Fig. 1.5.

In order to have available model compounds for compari-

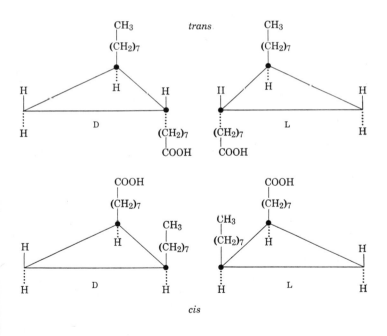

◆ Asymmetric carbon atoms

Fig. 1.5. The stereochemistry of 9,10-methyleneoctadecanoic acid.

son with lactobacillic acid, four long-chain fatty acids containing the cyclopropane ring—namely, racemic *cis* and *trans* 9,10-methyleneoctadecanoic acids and racemic *cis* and *trans* 11,12-methyleneoctadecanoic acids—were synthesized. The synthetic route to the *trans* series is illustrated on Fig. 1.6.

Trans-cyclopropane-1,2-dicarboxyclic acid (I) was selected as a logical starting point for preparation of acids of this series (20), since it is important to have available models of established stereo-structure for comparison with lactobacillic acid. The monomethyl ester chloride (II) of (I) is condensed with sodio ethyl acetoacetate, and the resulting crude diketo ester (III) on exposure to sodium methoxide in methanol gives methyl *trans*-γ-keto-α,β-methyleneadipate (IV) (21). Alkylation of (IV) with *n*-butyl iodide (V, $x = 5$) followed by saponification and decarboxylation gives *trans*-4-keto-2,3-methylenenonanoic acid (VI, $x = 5$), which is converted into *trans*-2,3-methylenenonanoic acid (VII, $x = 5$) by reduction with hydrazine. Alkylation of (IV) with *n*-hexyl iodide (V, $x = 7$) followed by saponification and reduction affords *trans*-2,3-methyleneundecanoic acid (VII, $x = 7$). A superior route to acids of structure (VII) involves condensation of ethyl diazoacetate (VIII) with olefins of the general structure (IX) followed by saponification of the resulting esters (X). Starting with octene-1 (IX, $x = 5$) and decene-1 (IX, $x = 7$), respectively, 2,3-methylenenonanoic acid (VII, $x = 5$) and 2,3-methyleneundecanoic acid (VII, $x = 7$) are obtained. Identity of the acids obtained by this route with the corresponding acids prepared from *trans*-cyclopropane-1,2-dicarboxylic acid (I) establishes their *trans* configuration.

For conversion into DL-*trans*-9,10-methyleneoctadecanoic acid, the acid chloride of (VII, $x = 7$) is converted into

Dear Librarian:

This book has been supplied without
Library of Congress Catalog Cards
because they are presently unavailable
and we did not want to delay shipment.

Bro-Dart Books, Inc.
P.O. Box 923
Williamsport, Pa.

methyl *trans*-3-keto-4,5-methylenetridecanoate (XI, $x = 7$) in the manner described for conversion of (II) into (IV). Alkylation of (XI, $x = 7$) with methyl ϵ-iodocaproate (XII, $y = 7$) followed by saponification and decarboxylation yields *trans*-8-keto-9,10-methyleneoctadecanoic acid (XIII, $x = 7$), which is reduced to DL-*trans*-9,10-methyleneoctadecanoic acid (XIV, x and $y = 7$). DL-*trans*-11,12-Methyleneoctadecanoic acid (XIV, $x = 5$, $y = 9$) is obtained from *trans*-2,3-methylenenonanoic acid (VII, $x = 5$) by the same sequence of reactions, with methyl *n*-iodocaprylate (XII, $y = 9$) serving as the alkylating reagent.

Comparison of the infrared absorption spectra of the highly purified synthetic acids with the spectrum of lactobacillic acid (Fig. 1.7) shows that the positions and intensities of the major absorption bands are identical. Especially noteworthy is the presence in all of the spectra of a sharp absorption band at 9.8 μ, which is characteristic of the cyclopropane ring. These findings, coupled with the chemical behavior of the synthetic acids (stability to oxidation and lability to hydrogenolysis with formation of nonadecanoic acid), provide convincing evidence for the proposed general architecture of lactobacillic acid. However, neither of the synthetic products is identical with lactobacillic acid from which they differ with respect to melting point, melting point of the amides, and most importantly as concerns the x-ray diffraction pattern (Table 1.2).

DL-*cis*-9,10-Methyleneoctadecanoic acid (dihydrosterculic acid) is an analog of lactobacillic acid which deserves particular attention. Its chemical behavior and infrared absorption spectrum are essentially identical with those of lactobacillic acid.

Dihydrosterculic acid is obtained when sterculic acid, a constituent of the seed fat of the tropical tree *Sterculia*

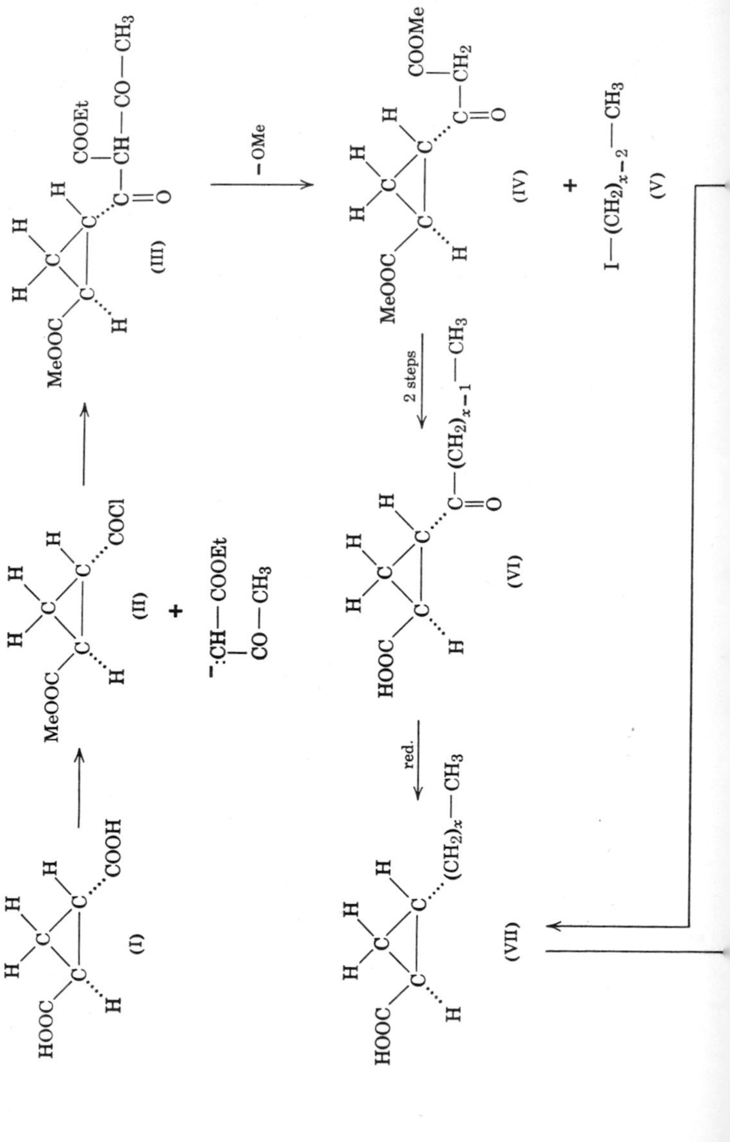
(I)
(II)
(III)
−OMe
(IV)
(V)
2 steps
(VI)
red.
(VII)

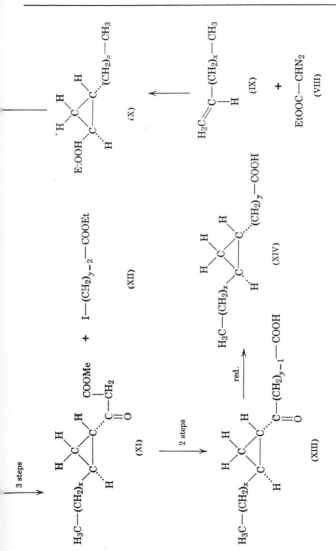

Fig. 1.6. Synthetic routes to cyclopropane fatty acids of the *trans* series.

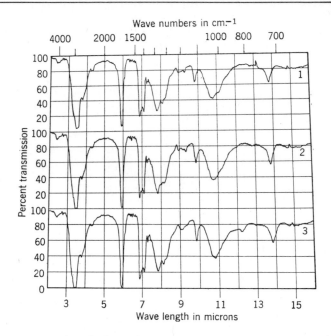

Fig. 1.7. Infrared absorption spectra of cyclopropane fatty acids. (1) DL-*trans*-11,12-Methyleneoctadecanoic acid. (2) DL-*trans*-9,10-Methyleneoctadecanoic acid. (3) Lactobacillic acid from *L. casei*.

foetida, is subjected to controlled catalytic hydrogenation (20, 22). The *cis* configuration for dihydrosterculic acid appeared likely, since low temperature catalytic hydrogenation of double bonds favors *cis* addition of hydrogen.

The chemical structure of sterculic acid and location of the three-membered ring is based on the reactions which are illustrated on Fig. 1.8 (22).

Since *cis-trans* isomers in the series of long-chain cyclopropane fatty acids differ little in the very physical properties

TABLE 1.2

Comparison of Certain Physical Properties of Naturally Occurring and Synthetic Cyclopropane Fatty Acids

Compound	Free Acid		Amide	
	Melting Point °C	Long Spacing Value Å	Melting Point °C	Long Spacing Value Å
Lactobacillic acid	28.0–29.0	41.0	80.0–82.0	37.5
Dihydrosterculic acid	39.7–40.5	43.9	86.4–87.6	37.7
DL-trans-9,10-Methyleneoctadecanoic acid	33.6–35.0	41.1	86.2–87.2	39.1
DL-trans-11,12-Methyleneoctadecanoic acid	36.5–37.2	41.3	84.0–85.0	39.1
DL-cis-9,10-Methyleneoctadecanoic acid	38.6–39.6	43.4	86.4–87.4	37.6
DL-cis-11,12-Methyleneoctadecanoic acid	31.0–33.6	43.3	84.0–85.2	39.3

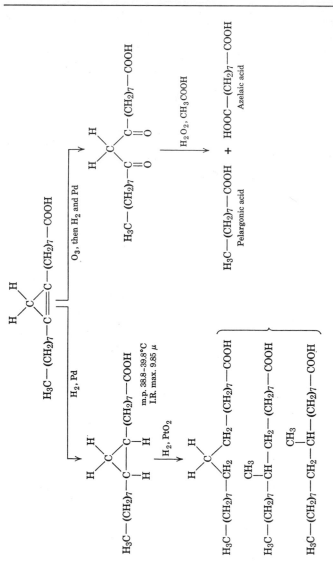

Fig. 1.8. Proof of structure of sterculic acid.

which are useful for purification purposes, methods for the synthesis of the *cis* cyclopropane fatty acids had to be devised which precluded the formation of mixtures of stereoisomers. Thus, an intermediate of unquestionable *cis* configuration had to be prepared which would lend itself to conversion into the desired long-chain cyclopropane fatty acids without any risk of *cis-trans* inversion during the process.

Cyclopropane-*cis*-1,2-diacetic acid, a compound not previously described, seemed ideally suited for this purpose, since methods are available for its conversion into the desired long-chain acids, and since the separation of its carboxyl groups from the centers of asymmetry eliminates the possibility for *cis-trans* inversions. Our route (23) to cyclopropane-*cis*-1,2-diacetic acid (Fig. 1.9) involves reaction of equimolar proportions of cyclohexa-1,4-diene (I) with dibromocarbene according to the method of Doering (24) to give the intermediate (II) which is readily converted by oxidation into (III). Cyclopropane-*cis*-1,2-diacetic acid is obtained in good yields when (III) is subjected to hydrogenolysis over a Raney nickel catalyst in presence of potassium hydroxide. The method of synthesis employed and the fact that cyclopropane-*cis*-1,2-diacetic acid, identical with the acid prepared by the above described scheme, can be obtained from cyclopropane-*cis*-1,2-dicarboxylic acid (25) leaves no doubt regarding the stereochemical configuration of this compound. For conversion into long-chain fatty acids, the carboxyl ends of cyclopropane-*cis*-1,2-diacetic acid are elongated through suitable manipulations (26, 27). For construction of the hydrocarbon end (Fig. 1.10), the diacetic acid (I) is converted into the monomethyl ester, and the acid chloride of the latter (II) is reacted with a suitable alkylcadmium reagent to form the keto acid (III), which is reduced with hydrazine to give an intermediate of structure (IV).

Elongation of the carboxyl end of intermediate (IV) (Fig. 1.11) is effected according to a scheme which was developed by Ställberg-Stenhagen (21). Identity of the synthetic compound (x and $y = 7$) with dihydrosterculic acid unequivocally establishes the structure of this compound as DL-*cis*-9,10-methyleneoctadecanoic acid. DL-*cis*-11,12-Methyleneoctadecanoic acid (DL-lactobacillic acid) is synthesized from cyclopropane diacetic acid by the same procedures.

Addition of iodomethyl zinc iodide across the double bond of olefins affords *cis* cyclopropane derivatives in high yield (28). This reaction has served to synthesize dihydro-

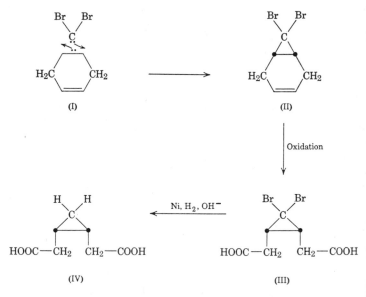

Fig. 1.9. Stereospecific synthesis of *cis*-cyclopropane-1,2-diacetic acid.

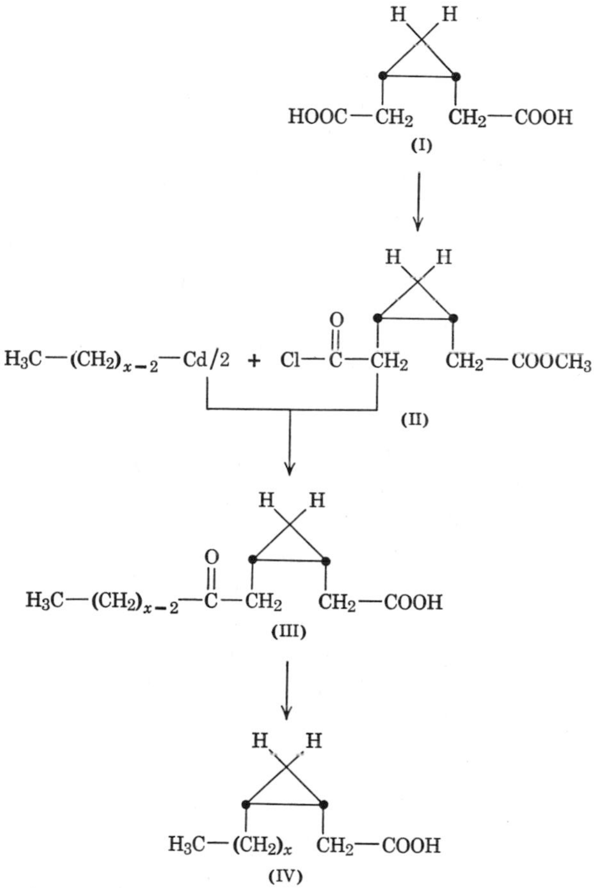

Intermediate for dihydrosterculic acid $x = 7$
Intermediate for DL-lactobacillic acid $x = 5$

Fig. 1.10. Elongation of hydrocarbon end.

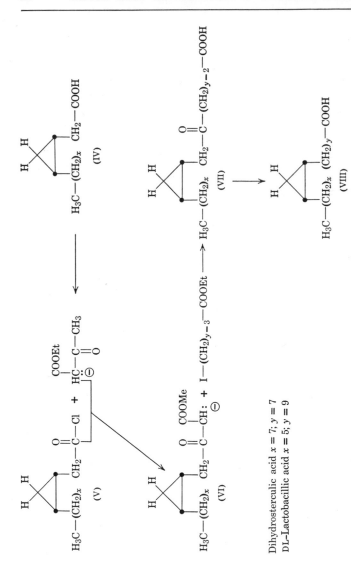

Fig. 1.11. Elongation of carboxyl end.

TABLE 1.3

Biotin-like Activity of Fatty Acids for Various Organisms

Biotin Equivalents (mμg.) per mg. of Fatty Acid

Fatty Acid	L. arabinosus	L. casei	L. delbrueckii	C. butyricum	L. acidophilus *
Oleic	5.6	5.4	39.2	2.9	(−)
Elaidic	8.2	6.4	10.4	(+)	1.0
Cis-vaccenic	5.0	4.6	21.8	3.3	(−)
Trans-vaccenic	7.6	3.4	(−)	(+)	1.7
(I)	3.7	5.6	15.5	(−)	1.5
(II)	3.6	4.8	21.6	(−)	(−)
(III)	2.7	4.6	3.7	(−)	(−)
(IV)	3.4	5.7	(−)	(−)	(−)

(+)   Slight growth (too low for accurate measurement).
(−)   No growth.
(I)   Lactobacillic acid.
(II)   Dihydrosterculic acid.
(III)   DL-*trans*-9,10-Methyleneoctadecanoic acid.
(IV)   DL-*trans*-11,12-Methyleneoctadecanoic acid.

21

* Synthetic *cis*-vaccenic acid served as the standard for these determinations, and its activity was arbitrarily chosen as unity.

sterculic acid (28) and DL-*cis*-9, 10-methylenehexadecanoic acid (29) from oleic and palmitoleic acids, respectively.

In Table 1.3, certain physical properties of both the *cis* and *trans* forms of synthetic racemic 9,10- and 11,12-methyleneoctadecanoic acids are compared with corresponding properties of lactobacillic and dihydrosterculic acids. DL-*cis*-11,12-Methyleneoctadecanoic acid is similar to, but not identical with, lactobacillic acid. The infrared absorption spectra of the synthetic *cis* acids match those of lactobacillic and dihydrosterculic acids.

4. X-RAY STUDIES OF CYCLOPROPANE FATTY ACIDS

Extensive x-ray crystallographic studies by Jeffrey et al. (30–32), using the above mentioned four synthetic racemic cyclopropane fatty acids, i.e., DL-*cis*- and *trans*-9,10-methyleneoctadecanoic and DL-*cis*- and *trans*-11,12-methyleneoctadecanoic acids, established the detailed stereochemistry of these molecules and contributed materially toward solution of the structure of lactobacillic acid. Two dimensional Fourier projections of DL-*cis*-11,12-methyleneoctadecanoic acid (left) and DL-*trans*-9,10-methyleneoctadecanoic acid (right) (Fig. 1.12) illustrate the striking difference in the shape of the *cis* and *trans* series of acids. The outstanding feature of the stereochemistry of the *cis* acids is the boomerang-like shape of the molecules with the bend about the cyclopropane ring. This is in marked contrast to the generally straight chain geometry of the *trans* acid. The arrangement of the molecules follows the head to head and tail to tail pattern, which is a characteristic feature of the crystal structure of long-chain fatty acids. Molecules of the

D and L configuration are hydrogen bonded into dimers through the centers of symmetry. The *trans* cyclopropane ring fits compactly into the regular arrangement of the methylene groups along the chain.

The unit cell dimensions of the DL-*cis*-9,10- and 11,12-acids and of the DL-*trans*-9,10- and 11,12-acids, respectively, are identical within the limits of the experimental procedures. The crystal lattices are nearly identical (isomorphous) because of the closely related arrangement of geometrically similar structural subunits. Single crystal and powder x-ray diffraction data show that dihydrosterculic and DL-*cis*-9,10-methyleneoctadecanoic acid are identical (30).

The crystal structure analysis of lactobacillic acid (33) carried to the stage of locating the carbon and oxygen atoms in one projection with sufficient precision to establish the general stereochemistry is shown on Fig. 1.13. Taken in conjunction with the chemical evidence (see Chapter 2, section 4) and the crystal structure analysis of the *cis*-11,12-methyleneoctadecanoic acid racemate (32) the electron density map provides conclusive evidence that lactobacillic acid is D or L *cis*-11,12-methyleneoctadecanoic acid. Individual molecules in the racemate and the naturally occurring species appear to have the same characteristic boomerang-like shape with the bend about the *cis* substituted cyclopropane ring, but the packing of individual molecules within the crystal lattice of the natural acid is significantly different from that which occurs in the synthetic racemate. The packing is less compact when all the molecules have the same sense as exemplified by the lower melting point and density (29° versus 37°; 0.97 g./cm.[3] versus 1.005 g./cm.[3]) of lactobacillic acid compared to DL-*cis*-11,12-methyleneocta-decanoic acid. In place of the centro symmetrically related left- and right-handed molecules which form the hydrogen-

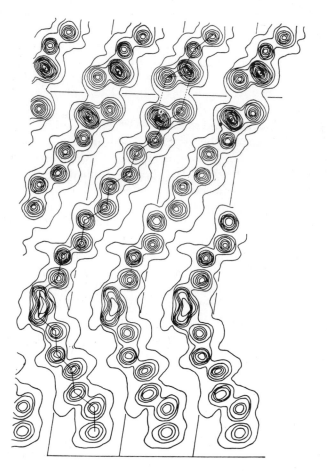

Fig. 1.12. Electron density maps of cyclopropane fatty acids. Left: DL-*cis*-11,12-Methyleneoctadecanoic acid. Right: DL-*trans*-9,10-Methyleneoctadecanoic acid.

612.397 H677

C.1

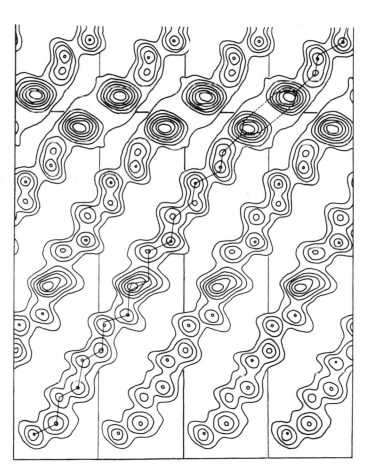

Fig. 1.12 *continued.*

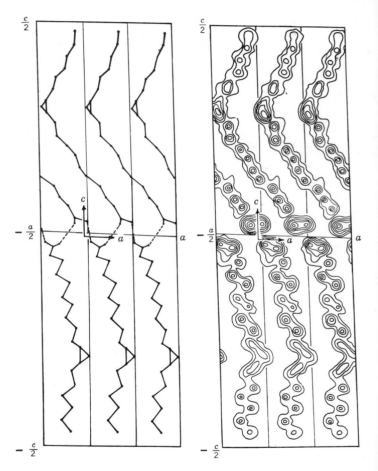

Fig. 1.13. Electron density map of lactobacillic acid.

bonded dimer in the racemate, an infinite sheet system of hydrogen bonds appears to link the carboxyl groups in the lactobacillic acid crystal (Fig. 1.13).

It is well-known that long-chain monocarboxylic acids exhibit trimorphism in both the odd and even series. In efforts to obtain crystals suitable for x-ray intensity measurements, a variety of solvents and conditions was employed, but in no instance was there any evidence for more than one crystal form of the cyclopropane acids. The acids crystallized from the melt give powder photographs which are of the same structure as those of the single crystals grown from solution. The cyclopropane ring appears to restrict the number of "economical" modes of packing the long chains into the crystal lattice.

Although synthesis of lactobacillic acid has not been achieved, there can be little doubt regarding the position of the cyclopropane ring and its *cis* configuration.

5. OCCURRENCE OF LACTOBACILLIC ACID AND ITS HOMOLOGS IN BACTERIA

Based on studies with radioactive tracers, O'Leary (34) suggested the presence of a C_{17} cyclopropane fatty acid in the lipids of an *Escherichia coli* mutant, and Dauchy and Asselineau (35) isolated an acid of this type from this organism. From an unidentified laboratory strain of *E. coli,* Kaneshiro and Marr (29) isolated a similar or possibly identical acid and provided convincing chemical evidence for the cyclopropane nature and the *cis*-9,10-location of the methylene bridge. Similar findings were reported by Innes Chalk and Kodicek (36). It is of interest to note that in addition to this cyclopropane acid, which accounts for some

20% of the fatty acids, the organism also contains lacto-bacillic acid. *Clostridium butyricum,* according to Bloch et al. (37), contains a family of cyclopropane fatty acids with 13, 15, 17, and 19 carbon atoms, respectively. Evidence for the presence in microorganisms of position isomeric methyleneoctadecanoic acids is presented in Chapter 3, section 3.

6. MICROBIOLOGICAL ACTIVITY OF CYCLOPROPANE FATTY ACIDS

The marked biotin-sparing activity of oleic acid in the nutrition of a variety of microorganisms, originally described by Williams and Fieger (1), was confirmed and extended by a number of investigators (2–7). These studies have shown that long-chain mono- and polyunsaturated fatty acids of both the *cis* and *trans* series have this biological property. Saturated fatty acids are inactive but may exert a synergistic effect when supplied to the organisms in conjunction with unsaturated acids (5). The *cis* isomers of a number of position and stereoisomeric monoethenoid octadecanoic acids exhibit practically the same biotin-sparing activity for *L. arabinosus* regardless of the position of the double bond. With exception of elaidic acid, which possesses a high degree of biotin-sparing potency, the *trans* isomers are less active than the corresponding *cis* forms, and the activity decreases in a stepwise manner, as the double bond is shifted from the center of the chain toward either the methyl or the carboxyl end (38). We find (39) that certain cyclopropane fatty acids share with the unsaturated fatty acids the ability to bring about microbial growth in presence of suboptimal quantities of biotin (Table 1.3).

Lactobacillus arabinosus and *L. casei* respond to unsaturated as well as cyclopropane fatty acids. With *L. casei,* the activity of the cyclopropane acids almost equals that of the unsaturated acids. The position (9,10 or 11,12) and stereochemistry (*cis* or *trans*) of the cyclopropane ring appears to exert little effect on the microbiological activity. *Lactobacillus delbrueckii* is more fastidious than *L. arabinosus* and *L. casei;* it responds well to oleic, *cis*-vaccenic, and elaidic acids, but grows poorly on *trans*-vaccenic acid. DL-*cis*-9,10-Methyleneoctadecanoic and lactobacillic acid are growth promoting; DL-*trans*-9,10-methyleneoctadecanoic acid exhibits a low order of activity and DL-*trans*-11,12-methyleneoctadecanoic acid is inactive. *Lactobacillus acidophilus* exhibits a marked preference for the *cis* isomers of the various fatty acids. It is stimulated by *cis*-vaccenic, lactobacillic and DL-*cis*-9,10-methyleneoctadecanoic acids, but fails to respond to the corresponding *trans* isomers, regardless of whether they are derived from unsaturated or cyclopropane fatty acids. Shifting of the ring from the 9,10- to the 11,12-position does not influence microbiological potency. The observation that *L. acidophilus* grows in presence of lactobacillic and DL-*cis*-9,10-methyleneoctadecanoic acid, but fails to respond to the *trans* isomers, provides biological support for the assigned *cis* configuration of lactobacillic acid. *Clostridium butyricum* responds to oleic, *cis*-vaccenic, linoleic, and linolenic acids but is not stimulated significantly by the other compounds. This result is unexpected, since the organisms contain both C_{17} and C_{19} cyclopropane fatty acids (37).

Based on this experimental evidence, it must be concluded that certain long-chain cyclopropane fatty acids share with long-chain unsaturated fatty acids the ability to promote growth of certain microorganisms in the presence of suboptimal amounts of biotin.

REFERENCES

1. Williams, V. R., and E. A. Fieger, *J. Biol. Chem.*, **166**, 335 (1946).
2. Hofmann, K., and A. E. Axelrod, *Arch. Biochem.*, **14**, 482 (1947).
3. Axelrod, A. E., K. Hofmann, and B. F. Daubert, *J. Biol. Chem.*, **169**, 761 (1947).
4. Williams, W. L., H. P. Broquist, and E. E. Snell, *J. Biol. Chem.*, **170**, 619 (1947).
5. Axelrod, A. E., M. Mitz, and K. Hofmann, *J. Biol. Chem.*, **175**, 265 (1948).
6. Shull, G. M., and W. H. Peterson, *Arch. Biochem.*, **18**, 69 (1948).
7. Shull, G. M., R. W. Thoma, and W. H. Peterson, *Arch. Biochem.*, **20**, 227 (1949).
8. Hofmann, K., and R. A. Lucas, *J. Am. Chem. Soc.*, **72**, 4328 (1950).
9. Hofmann, K., R. A. Lucas, and S. M. Sax, *J. Biol. Chem.*, **195**, 473 (1952).
10. Hofmann, K., and S. M. Sax, *J. Biol. Chem.*, **205**, 55 (1953).
11. Hofmann, K., and F. Tausig, *J. Biol. Chem.*, **213**, 425 (1955).
12. Hofmann, K., and F. Tausig, *J. Biol. Chem.*, **213**, 415 (1955).
13. Chargaff, E., and M. Levine, *J. Biol. Chem.*, **124**, 195 (1938).
14. Geiger, W. B., Jr., and R. J. Anderson, *J. Biol. Chem.*, **129**, 519 (1939).
15. Velick, S. F., and R. J. Anderson, *J. Biol. Chem.*, **152**, 523 (1944).
16. Velick, S. F., *J. Biol. Chem.*, **152**, 533 (1944).
17. Velick, S. F., *J. Biol. Chem.*, **156**, 101 (1944).
18. Kaneshiro, T., and A. G. Marr, *J. Lipid Research*, **3**, 184 (1962).
19. Derfer, J. M., E. E. Pickett, and C. E. Boord, *J. Am. Chem. Soc.*, **71**, 2482 (1949).
20. Hofmann, K., O. Jucker, W. R. Miller, A. C. Young, Jr., and F. Tausig, *J. Am. Chem. Soc.*, **76**, 1799 (1954).
21. Ställberg-Stenhagen, S., *Archiv. Kemi. Mineral Geol.*, **A22**, No. 19, 11 (1946).
22. Nunn, J. R., *J. Chem. Soc.*, 313 (1952).

23. Hofmann, K., S. F. Orochena, S. M. Sax, and G. A. Jeffrey, *J. Am. Chem. Soc.*, **81**, 992 (1959).
24. Doering, W. von E., and A. K. Hoffmann, *J. Am. Chem. Soc.*, **76**, 6162 (1954).
25. Vogel, E., K. H. Ott, and K. Gajer, *Ann. Chem.*, **644**, 172 (1961).
26. Hofmann, K., S. F. Orochena, and C. W. Yoho, *J. Am. Chem. Soc.*, **79**, 3608 (1957).
27. Hofmann, K., and C. W. Yoho, *J. Am. Chem. Soc.*, **81**, 3356 (1959).
28. Simmons, H. E., and R. D. Smith, *J. Am. Chem. Soc.*, **81**, 4256 (1959).
29. Kaneshiro, T., and A. G. Marr, *J. Biol. Chem.*, **236**, 2615 (1961).
30. Brotherton, T., and G. A. Jeffrey, *J. Am. Chem. Soc.*, **79**, 5132 (1957).
31. Brotherton, T., B. Craven, and G. A. Jeffrey, *Acta Cryst.*, **11**, 546 (1958).
32. Craven, B., and G. A. Jeffrey, *Acta Cryst.*, **12**, 754 (1959).
33. Craven, B., and G. A. Jeffrey, *J. Am. Chem. Soc.*, **82**, 3858 (1960).
34. O'Leary, W. M., *J. Bact.*, **78**, 709 (1959).
35. Dauchy, S., and J. Asselineau, *Compt. Rend. Acad. Sci.*, Paris, **250**, 2635 (1960).
36. Innes Chalk, K. J., and E. Kodicek, *Biochem. Biophys. Acta*, **50**, 579 (1961).
37. Goldfine, H., and K. Bloch, *J. Biol. Chem.*, **236**, 2596 (1961).
38. Cheng, A. L. S., S. M. Greenberg, H. J. Deuel, Jr., and D. Melnick, *J. Biol. Chem.*, **192**, 611 (1951).
39. Hofmann, K., and C. Panos, *J. Biol. Chem.*, **210**, 687 (1954).

2

BIOSYNTHESIS OF CYCLOPROPANE FATTY ACIDS

1. ESTIMATION OF THE FATTY ACID COMPOSITION OF BACTERIAL LIPIDS

A method for the quantitative estimation of individual fatty acids in small samples of bacterial lipids was required to permit insight into the metabolic interplay among various fatty acids in bacterial metabolism.

In 1950, Bolding (1) devised a chromatographic microtechnique for determining the composition of mixtures of straight-chain saturated fatty acids. This procedure was modified in our laboratory (2) and applied to the simultaneous determination of monoethenoid, saturated, and branched chain fatty acids as they occur in the lipids of certain microorganisms. The method involves (1) isolation of the fatty acids from the acid autoclaved cells, (2) hydroxylation of the fatty acid mixture with performic acid, (3) separation of the resulting mixture of hydroxylated fatty acids by reversed phase chromatography on rubber columns, and (4) microbiological determination of lactobacillic acid in the stearic-lactobacillic acid fraction derived from chromatography. Acetone-water mixtures of increasing acetone content serve as eluant for the various fatty acids. The initial hydroxylation step converts the monoethenoid fatty acids, mainly *cis*-vaccenic acid, into the corresponding dihydroxy derivatives. In contrast to the unsaturated acids, which cannot be cleanly separated from the saturates by rubber chromatography, the dihydroxy acids evolve from the column with the eluants of the lowest acetone content and are thus readily separable from the saturated acids and lactobacillic acid. This "dihydroxy" fraction is a measure of the proportion of unsaturated fatty acids both C_{16} and C_{18} in the bacterial lipids. A typical chromatogram obtained with a synthetic mixture of fatty acids relating fraction number to the volume of $0.01N$ sodium hydroxide required to titrate each fraction to the phenolphthalein endpoint is illustrated in Fig. 2.1. In this experiment the recovery of individual fatty acids ranged from 81 to 110% of theory. Lactobacillic and stearic acids evolve from the column as a single inseparable peak. The lactobacillic acid content of this fraction is readily determined by microbiological assay with *L. delbrueckii*. A typical curve relating lactobacillic acid content of the medium and cell growth is illustrated on Fig. 2.2. The studies which are summarized on Table 2.1 demonstrate conclusively that addition of stearic acid to the lactobacillic acid samples does not interfere with the biological assay. Verification of this point was of considerable importance since saturated fatty acids may increase synergistically the growth promoting potency of certain unsaturated fatty acids (3).

Gas-liquid chromatography of the methyl esters of bacterial fatty acids (4, 5, 6) has largely replaced the older procedure, since it offers significant advantages in speed,

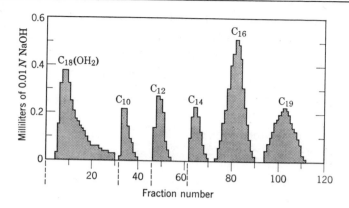

Fig. 2.1. Chromatographic pattern of a synthetic fatty acid mixture (47.8 mg.), composed of: oleic acid, 17.6 mg. (81%); capric acid, 1.6 mg. (103%); lauric acid, 2.2 mg. (110%); myristic acid, 2.5 mg. (96%); palmitic acid, 13.0 mg. (98%); lactobacillic acid, 10.9 mg. (97%). The figures in parentheses represent recoveries from the column. Solvents were changed at the positions indicated by the dotted lines.

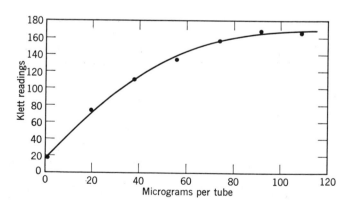

Fig. 2.2. Lactobacillic acid growth curve determined with *L. delbrueckii.*

TABLE 2.1

Microbiological Determination of Lactobacillic Acid in the Presence of Stearic Acid

Material Assayed	Lactobacillic Acid	
	Found	Recovery
Stearic Acid mg.	Inactive mg.	%
S (0.0) + L (3.6)	3.6; 3.9	100; 110
S (1.0) + L (5.7)	5.3; 5.3	93; 93
S (1.8) + L (2.8)	2.9; 2.9	105; 105
S (2.5) + L (2.5)	2.6; 2.7	106; 109
S (4.0) + L (1.0)	1.0; 0.9	100; 90

convenience, accuracy, and the amount of material required. However, the fundamental observations which led to recognition of the biosynthetic route to lactobacillic acid were based on the use of reversed phase chromatography on rubber as outlined in this section.

2. CHEMICAL NATURE OF THE MONOETHENOID FATTY ACIDS IN MICROORGANISMS

Oleic acid has been reported to be a constituent of the lipids of many microorganisms. Its presence has been inferred from the isolation of stearic acid on hydrogenation, and from iodine numbers obtained prior to hydrogenation. Careful structure analyses of the monoethenoid octadecanoic acid from *L. arabinosus* and *L. casei* led to its identification as *cis*-vaccenic acid (*cis*-11-octadecenoic acid) (7, 8). The melting points of *cis*-vaccenic acid and oleic acid and a number of their derivatives exhibit a striking similarity

(Table 2.2); consequently, great care must be exercised in the identification of monoethenoid octadecanoic acids of bacterial origin. Characterization of such acids may be achieved by (1) conversion into the respective dihydroxy derivatives, (2) oxidative cleavage of the latter and identification of the fragments, and (3) preparation of a number of derivatives and comparison with corresponding derivatives of established identity. Since the x-ray diffraction patterns of the dihydroxy derivatives of isomeric octadecenoic acids exhibit characteristic differences (9), this property also is useful in establishing the position of the double bond.

Gas-liquid chromatography allows identification of the oxidative split products derived from position isomeric monounsaturated fatty acids containing 16 and 18 carbon atoms, respectively, as they occur in bacterial lipids and makes possible the simultaneous identification of the double-bond position in both classes of acids on a micro scale (4, 10).

By this procedure, it was shown conclusively that in addition to its presence in *L. arabinosus,* where it was discovered, *cis*-vaccenic acid is widely distributed in bacteria. It occurs as the sole monoethenoid octadecanoic acid in *L. casei* and mixtures of *cis*-vaccenic acid and of oleic acid are present in the lipids of a *Streptococcus* species, in *E. coli* (6) (70% *cis*-vaccenic, 30% oleic acid), in *A. tumefaciens* (10) (90% *cis*-vaccenic, 10% oleic acid), in *Azotobacter agilis* (10) (80% *cis*-vaccenic, 20% oleic acid), and in *C. butyricum* (63% *cis*-vaccenic, 37% oleic acid). Palmitoleic acid (*cis*-9,10-hexadecenoic acid) is contained in the lipids of *E. coli* (6), *L. planarum, A. tumefaciens,* and *A. agilis* (10). Isomers of this acid differing in the location of the double bond are present in a *Streptococcus* species (11) (*cis*-11,12-hexadecanoic acid) and in *C. butyricum.* The C_{16} unsaturated frac-

TABLE 2.2

Comparison of Melting Points of *L. casei* C$_{18}$ Liquid Fatty Acid, *Cis*-Vaccenic Acid, and Oleic Acid, and of Their Derivatives

Derivative	*L. casei* Acid (A) °C	*Cis*-Vaccenic Acid (Synthetic) (B) °C	Oleic Acid (C) °C	(A) + (B) (1:1 Mixture) °C	(A) + (C) (1:1 Mixture) °C
Free acid (*cis*)	13.4–14.4	12.4–13.0	12.5–13.0	12.4–13.2	−2.0–+1.9
Low melting dihydroxy	91.4–93.2	92.2–94.0	91.8–93.8	91.4–93.0	80.4–85.0
Amide	79.0–80.8	78.0–80.0	74.6–75.4	78.0–80.3	72.8–74.2
p-Phenylphenacyl ester	65.6–66.8	65.0–66.2	58.4–60.6	65.0–66.0	55.0–58.2
Oxirane	45.8–47.3	46.0–47.6	57.0–58.0	46.0–47.2	43.5–47.0
Isomerized acid (*trans*)	42.4–43.5	42.5–44.1	42.6–44.0	42.3–44.0	36.0–38.5

tion of the latter organism consists of a mixture of *cis*-9,10-hexadecenoic and *cis*-7,8-hexadecenoic acids (12, 13). Several strains of tubercle bacillus (4) and *Mycobacterium phlei* contain oleic acid as the sole monounsaturated C_{18} component. Polyunsaturated fatty acids do not occur in these various microorganisms (14).

3. FATTY ACID INTERCONVERSIONS IN LACTOBACILLI

The first clue pertaining to a close metabolic relation between *cis*-vaccenic and lactobacillic acids came from the results (15) recorded on Table 2.3 which illustrate the effect of variations in the growth medium on the fatty acid spectrum of *L. delbrueckii*. Since this organism requires Tween 40 (sorbitan monopalmitate) for maximal growth in presence of unsaturated fatty acids (16), information on the effect of Tween 40 on the fatty acid spectrum is important. Comparison of the biotin cells (culture I) with the biotin plus Tween 40 cells (culture II) shows the total fatty acid content of the latter to be almost twice that of the former. Inspection of the fatty acid spectrum reveals a markedly higher palmitic acid content of the Tween cells, but an increase in the (C_{18} plus C_{19}) and in the C_{19} fraction is also observed. The "dihydroxy" fraction is lower than that of the controls. Adsorption to the cell surface of palmitic acid, derived from the Tween, may explain the high palmitic acid content of the culture II cells, but the increase in other fatty acids is hardly explicable along these lines. It appears likely that, in addition to providing the organisms with a source of palmitic acid, the Tween stimulates fatty acid biosynthesis.

TABLE 2.3

Fatty Acid Composition of *L. delbrueckii* Cells Cultivated on Various Media

Culture Number	Percent Total Fatty Acids	Biotin Content µg. per g.	Composition of Total Fatty Acids, Percent								Percent Recovery
			Dihydroxy	C_{10}	C_{12}	C_{14}	C_{16}	$C_{18}+C_{19}$	C_{18}	C_{19}	
I	1.8	1.3	45.5	0.5	1.1	2.5	27.5	17.2	10.8	6.4	94.3
II	3.3	1.7	19.8	1.3	1.5	2.9	45.8	23.8	14.4	9.4	95.1
III	3.6	<0.1	24.9	1.2	1.6	3.5	46.2	16.9		27.3	94.3
IV	2.9	<0.1	24.3	0.7	2.0	1.4	38.5	20.6	2.3	18.3	87.5
V	2.6	<0.1	Nil	Trace	2.0	2.4	42.0	41.3	8.7	32.6	85.7

The following additions, per liter of basal medium (15), were made to grow the various batches of cells: culture I, 3 µg. of biotin; culture II, 3 µg. of biotin plus 1.4 g. of Tween 40; culture III, 40 mg. of oleic acid plus 1.4 g. of Tween 40; culture IV, 62.2 mg. of *cis*-vaccenic acid plus 1.4 g. of Tween 40; culture V, 46.8 mg. of lactobacillic acid plus 1.4 g. of Tween 40.

The biotin content of the cells which are grown on the various fatty acids (cultures III to V) is significantly lower than that of the cells grown in the presence of biotin (cultures I and II). Thus, the growth-promoting potency of unsaturated or cyclopropane fatty acids is not explicable in terms of their serving as precursors for biotin biosynthesis. Trace amounts of biotin (below the limits amenable to quantitative determination) are always present in the fatty acid grown cells; however, the metabolic role of these trace levels of biotin is difficult to evaluate. Substitution of biotin by *cis*-vaccenic acid (culture IV), although not affecting significantly the "dihydroxy" acid level, practically doubles the C_{19} acid content of the bacteria. Most remarkable is the composition of the fatty acid mixture of the lactobacillic acid grown cells (culture V). The lipids of these cells are completely devoid of unsaturated fatty acids, as reflected by the absence of "dihydroxy" fatty acids. As is to be expected, the (C_{18} plus C_{19}) and the C_{19} content of these lipids is markedly higher than in the biotin cells.

Lactobacillic acid grown cells of *L. arabinosus* and *L. casei* (17) (Table 2.4) are also free of unsaturated fatty acids. Biotin grown cells of these organisms contain a sizable "dihydroxy" fraction.

Lactobacillic acid appears to possess the ability to substitute for *cis*-vaccenic acid in the metabolism of all three organisms. We concluded from these findings (15) that "the biosynthesis of lactobacillic acid may involve the addition of a 'C_1' fragment to the double bond of *cis*-vaccenic acid." Experiments with labeled *cis*-vaccenic acid and labeled one-carbon donors, to be discussed in Chapter 2, section 5, validate our hypothesis.

TABLE 2.4

Fatty Acid Composition of *L. arabinosus* and *L. casei* Cells Cultivated on Various Media

Organism	Culture Number	Total Fatty Acids	Dihydroxy	C_{10}	C_{12}	C_{14}	C_{16}	C_{18}	C_{19}
					Composition of Total Fatty Acids				
L. arabinosus	I	3.0	6.8	0.3	3.4	1.5	44.0	6.6	27.7
	II	3.8	nil	trace	trace	trace	52.7	4.9	39.3
L. casei	I	2.3	20.5	1.0	0.5	6.3	60.4	6.5	12.8
	II	2.9	nil	trace	trace	8.4	49.5	5.2	41.2

The following additions, per liter of basal medium (17), were made to grow the various batches of cells for lipid analyses:

L. arabinosus culture I, 0.5 μg. of biotin plus 1.2 g. of Tween 40; culture II, 5 mμg. of biotin plus 1.2 g. ot Tween 40 plus 55 mg. of lactobacillic acid.

L. casei culture I, 1 μg. of biotin plus 1.2 g. of Tween 40; culture II, 45 mg. of lactobacillic acid plus 1.2 g. of Tween 40.

41

4. POSITION OF THE CYCLOPROPANE RING IN LACTOBACILLIC ACID AND SEPARATION OF CARBON ATOM 19 FROM THE MOLECULE

As has been mentioned previously (Chapter 1, section 2), lactobacillic acid reacts readily with hydrogen bromide with formation of a mixture of monobromononadecanoic acids which arise from addition of the elements of hydrogen bromide to the cyclopropane ring. Dihydrosterculic, DL-*trans*-9,10-methylene- and DL-*trans*-11,12-methyleneoctadecanoic acids exhibit the same behavior (18). Four structural possibilities, A, B, C, and D (Fig. 2.3), must be considered for the ring opening products. However, structures C and D appear to represent the most likely ones. The ring opened compounds derived from the two synthetic *trans* acids, from lactobacillic acid and from dihydrosterculic acid separately were dehydrobrominated by exposure to boiling collidine. In this manner each bromo acid was converted into a mixture of olefinic acids which may contain some or all of the components shown on Fig. 2.3.

The crude dehydrohalogenation products from each acid were then oxidized by the Lemieux procedure (19) and the mixture of oxidation products separated into a neutral and an acidic fraction. The latter was analyzed for its various components by chromatography on buffered silica-gel columns (20). The experimental conditions employed for analysis were so selected that the dibasic acids could be sharply separated, whereas monocarboxylic acids evolved at the very beginning of the column development as a single unresolved peak. The nature of the dibasic oxidation products provided important insight into the position of the cyclopropane ring in the original acid. As is apparent from inspection of the patterns shown on Fig. 2.4, the

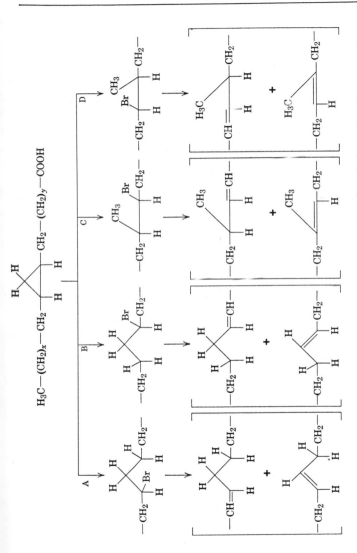

Fig. 2.3. Monounsaturated acids which may result from the degradation of cyclopropane fatty acids.

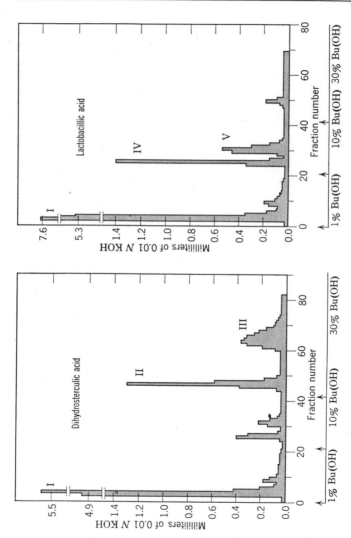

Fig. 2.4. Chromatographic separation on buffered silicic acid columns of dibasic acids from degradation of long-chain fatty acids containing the cyclopropane ring. Peak I, monocarboxylic acids.

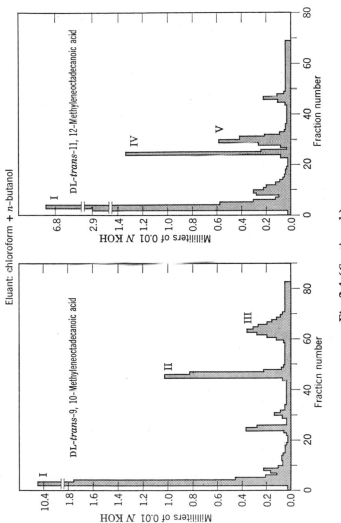

Fig. 2.4 (Continued.)

dibasic acids derived from the degradation of *trans*-9,10-methyleneoctadecanoic acid (mainly azelaic acid plus suberic acid) differ markedly from those resulting from degradation of *trans*-11,12-methyleneoctadecanoic acid (undecanedioic acid plus sebacic acid). The acids corresponding to each chromatographic peak were isolated and their identity verified by melting point, by mixed melting point with an authentic sample, and by x-ray diffraction measurements.

The finding that the dibasic acid pattern derived from the degradation of dihydrosterculic acid matches that obtained from *trans*-9,10-methyleneoctadecanoic acid; whereas that derived from degradation of lactobacillic acid duplicates essentially that obtained from *trans*-11,12-methyleneoctadecanoic acid establishes the position of the cyclopropane ring in these acids.

The experiences with this type of degradation (Fig. 2.5), indicate that the major route follows the pathways marked by heavy lines.

In addition to providing information regarding the ring position, the above mentioned degradative scheme allows the selective removal of the methylene bridge carbon atom from the rest of the carbon chain. Oxidation with hypoiodite of the total mixture of neutral and acidic products derived from the oxidative degradation yields iodoform. Only two of the many plausible oxidative fragments, namely compounds I and II, can be precursors of this compound. Since the ketone methyl groups of these products originate from the methylene bridge carbon of the original compound, the iodoform carbon is likewise derived from this source. The implications of this in the elucidation of the biosynthesis of lactobacillic acid will be discussed in the following section.

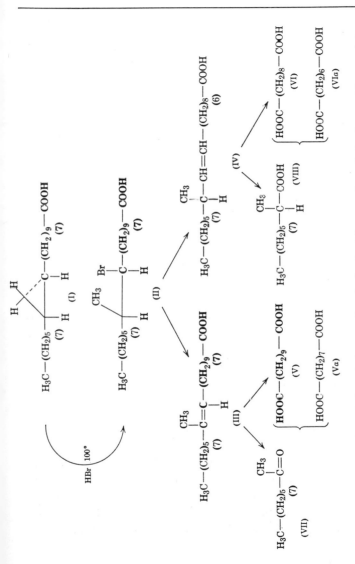

Fig. 2.5. Interpretation of degradation results obtained with some long-chain fatty acids containing the cyclopropane ring.

$$\begin{array}{cc} \overset{\displaystyle CH_3}{\underset{\displaystyle |}{}} & \overset{\displaystyle CH_3}{\underset{\displaystyle |}{}} \\ H_3C-(CH_2)_x-CO & OC-(CH_2)_y-COOH \\ \text{(I)} & \text{(II)} \end{array}$$

The gas-liquid chromatographic identification of the methyl ketones resulting from the chromic trioxide oxidation of the products of hydrogenolysis (Fig. 1.3; structure III) provides another means for locating the position of the methylene bridge in cyclopropane fatty acids. Thus, the formation of a mixture of 2-nonanone and 2-octanone on oxidation of the hydrogenolysis products derived from a methylenehexadecanoic acid from an *E. coli* species locates the methylene bridge between positions 9 and 10 (6). These experimental results corroborate fully the assumption, stated in Chapter 1, section 2, that the hydrogenolysis of cyclopropane fatty acids brings about formation of an inseparable mixture of methyl branched fatty acids plus that straight chain fatty acid containing the same number of carbon atoms as the original compound.

5. CYCLOPROPANE RING BIOSYNTHESIS

Studies on fatty acid interconversions in lactic acid organisms which were presented in Chapter 2, section 3, suggested a close metabolic relation between *cis*-vaccenic acid on the one hand and lactobacillic acid on the other.

Experiments to be discussed in this section demonstrate that the biosynthesis of lactobacillic acid in *L. arabinosus* proceeds in the manner illustrated in Fig. 2.6. A one-carbon fragment, through as yet unelucidated mechanisms, is added across the double bond of *cis*-vaccenic acid which provides the source for the entire carbon chain of the

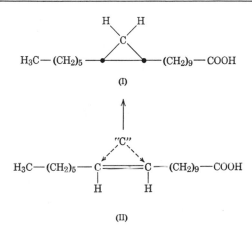

Fig. 2.6. Biosynthetic route to lactobacillic acid.

lactobacillic acid molecule. The experimental evidence for this rather novel biochemical reaction stems from studies on the distribution of radioactivity in individual fatty acids isolated from *L. arabinosus* grown on such various radioactive precursors as *cis*-vaccenic acid-1-C^{14}, methionine methyl-C^{14}, and formate-C^{14}, respectively (21, 22). In experiments in which the bacteria grow on media low in biotin in presence of carboxyl labeled *cis*-vaccenic acid (6.72×10^6 c.p.m.), 1.26×10^6 c.p.m. or 18.7% of the radioactivity is associated with the cells. The distribution of label among the various fractions (Table 2.5) shows that 99.2% of this radioactivity is located in the fatty acid fraction; the other cellular constituents are practically inactive. The major proportion of activity is located in the unsaturated ("dihydroxy") fatty acid and lactobacillic acid fractions; capric, lauric, myristic, and palmitic acids and the nonsaponifiable material show negligible labeling (Table 2.6). The specific activity of the "dihydroxy" (1.10×10^7

TABLE 2.5

Distribution of Radioactivity in Fractions from *L. arabinosus* Cells Grown on Various Radioactive Precursors

	Cis-Vaccenic Acid-1-C^{14}		Methionine-Methyl-C^{14}		Formate-C^{14} *		Formate-C^{14} †	
	Total c.p.m.	%	Total c.p.m.	%	Total c.p.m.	%	Total c.p.m.	%
Hydrolyzed cells	1.26×10^6	100	3.15×10^7	100	9.22×10^5	100	1.15×10^6	100
Ether-extracted hydrolyzed cells	0.01×10^6	0.8	2.20×10^7	69.8	9.20×10^5	99.7	1.13×10^6	98.3
Mixed fatty acids	1.25×10^6	99.2	0.95×10^7	30.2	0.02×10^5	0.2	0.02×10^3	0.2
Nonsaponifiable material	Trace		Trace		Trace		Trace	

* Grown in medium containing formate-C^{14}.

† Cells suspended in medium containing formate-C^{14}.

TABLE 2.6

Incorporation of Labeled Precursors into *L. arabinosus* Fatty Acids

Acids	Cis-Vaccenic Acid-1-C^{14}			Methionine-Methyl-C^{14}			Formate-C^{14} *		
	Cellular Acids (%)	c.p.m./mmole	Distribution of Radioactivity (%)	Cellular Acids (%)	c.p.m./mmole	Distribution of Radioactivity (%)	Cellular Acids (%)	c.p.m./mmole	Distribution of Radioactivity (%)
"Dihydroxy"	15.3	1.10 × 10^7	24.1	15.3	0.16 × 10^7	0.7	17.8	3.93 × 10^4	39.1
Capric	0.2	...†	...	0.6	0.56 × 10^7	0.2	0.2	...†	...
Lauric	0.2	...†	...	0.8	0.39 × 10^7	0.2	0.5	...†	...
Myristic	0.8	...†	...	1.0	0.41 × 10^7	0.2	0.6	...†	...
Palmitic	41.8	...†	...	46.0	0.12 × 10^7	2.0	39.6	...†	...
Lactobacillic	31.4	1.25 × 10^7	69.9	33.8	9.65 × 10^7	95.5	36.5	2.76 × 10^4	57.1
Total recovery	89.7	...	94.0	97.5	...	99.8	95.2	...	96.2

* Cells suspended in medium containing formate-C^{14}.

† Not significantly above background.

c.p.m./mmole) and that of the lactobacillic acid fraction (1.25×10^7 c.p.m./mmole), which corresponds to 82 and 92% respectively of that of the added *cis*-vaccenic acid (specific activity 1.35×10^7 c.p.m./mmole), demonstrates conclusively that lactobacillic acid is indeed formed from *cis*-vaccenic acid. The results show further that there is little degradation or redistribution of *cis*-vaccenic acid carboxyl carbon under the conditions employed in these experiments.

In the studies with one-carbon donors methionine-C^{14} (2.69×10^7 c.p.m.) or sodium formate-C^{14} (7.57×10^6 c.p.m.) were added with 40 mg. of nonlabeled *cis*-vaccenic acid per liter of medium. Cells grown in 3.5 liters of medium were analyzed. In the experiments with cell suspensions, bacterial cells grown in 1 liter of medium, fortified with 40 mg. of nonradioactive *cis*-vaccenic acid, were harvested and washed with 0.85% sodium chloride solution. The bacteria were then suspended in 10 volumes of $0.03M$ potassium dihydrogen phosphate (pH 6.8) containing 1% of glucose and sodium formate-C^{14} (1.20×10^7 c.p.m.) and incubated at 37° for 24 hours with occasional shaking.

Methionine-methyl-C^{14} is effectively incorporated into the bacterial cells which contain 3.15×10^7 c.p.m. or 33.4% of the added radioactivity (Table 2.5). In contrast to the observations with *cis*-vaccenic acid, 69.8% of the label is located in the nonlipid fractions, the remaining radioactivity being present in the mixed fatty acids (Table 2.5). The bulk of the radioactivity (96.5%) in the mixed fatty acids is located in the lactobacillic acid; the other fatty acids exhibit a very low degree of labeling (Table 2.6). Incorporation of formate carbon into the bacterial cells is low under both sets of experimental conditions. Only 3.5% of the added radioactivity is incorporated into the growing cells; the incorporation into the resting cells is 9.6%. The mixed fatty acids show little labeling in contrast to other cellular constituents which contain between 98.3 and 99.7% of the radioactivity (Table 2.5). The label present in the mixed fatty acids is distributed in the main between the "dihydroxy" and lactobacillic acid fractions (Table 2.6).

Samples of biosynthetically labeled lactobacillic acid from the methionine and formate experiments were degraded in the manner described, and the specific activity of the resulting iodoform was recorded. As has been mentioned previously, in this scheme of degradation the iodoform carbon is derived exclusively from the methylene bridge carbon of the lactobacillic acid molecule. The observation (Table 2.7) that the specific activity of the iodoform is 84% that of the lactobacillic acid in the methionine experiment and 80% that of lactobacillic acid in the formate experiment demonstrates conclusively that the methylene bridge carbon of the lactobacillic acid molecule is derived from one-carbon fragments.

O'Leary (23, 24) working with *L. arabinosus* also demonstrated incorporation of *cis*-vaccenic acid-l-C^{14} and of me-

TABLE 2.7

Radioactivity of Iodoform-C^{14} Obtained from Biosynthetic C^{14} Lactobacillic Acid

	C^{14}-Formate Experiment dis./min./mmole	Methionine- Methyl-C^{14} Experiment dis./min./mmole
Lactobacillic acid	3464	22350
Iodoform	2767 *	18787 *

* The iodoform was purified to constant radioactivity.

thionine-methyl-C^{14} into the lactobacillic acid molecule, but he did not elucidate the exact position of the label. In their use of gas chromatography for separation of fatty acids, Innes Chalk and Kodicek (25) observed incorporation of methionine-methyl-C^{14} into lactobacillic acid with *E. coli* and *L. casei*. In *L. casei* all the label was located in the lactobacillic acid, which is the sole cyclopropane fatty acid present. In *E. coli* which contains both lactobacillic acid and its lower homolog *cis*-9,10-methylenehexadecanoic acid, the label was distributed between these acids in the proportion 42 to 58%. Incorporation of methionine-methyl into *cis*-9,10-methyleneoctadecanoic acid had been demonstrated earlier (24). Although the exact position of the label in the lower homolog of lactobacillic acid has not been established by degradation, it appears very likely that it is located in the methylene bridge carbon. Addition of unlabeled formate to the growth medium of *L. casei* does not affect incorporation of methionine-methyl-C^{14} into the lactobacillic acid molecule. Thus, the methyl group of methionine is probably not incorporated into lactobacillic acid via oxidation to "active formate" (25).

The biosynthesis of 10-methylstearic acid from oleic acid, which represents a major metabolic reaction of the latter acid in *Mycobacterium phlei* (14), appears to be related intimately to lactobacillic acid formation. However, there is no net change in the oxidation state in lactobacillic acid biosynthesis—in contrast to 10-methylstearic acid formation, which must involve a reductive step. The methyl group of methionine serves as the source for the extra carbon in both processes.

Addition of one-carbon fragments to double bonds provides a general biochemical mechanism for formation of branched-chain compounds not only in the long-chain fatty acid series but also with sterols. The methyl group in position 28 of ergosterol derives from methionine methyl (26, 27) and is probably introduced via related routes.

REFERENCES

1. Boldingh, J., *Rec. Trav. Chim. Pays Bas,* **69,** 247 (1950).
2. Hofmann, K., C. Y. Hsiao, D. B. Henis, and C. Panos, *J. Biol. Chem.,* **217,** 49 (1955).
3. Axelrod, A. E., M. Mitz, and K. Hofmann, *J. Biol. Chem.,* **175,** 265 (1948).
4. Cason, J., and P. Tavs, *J. Biol. Chem.,* **234,** 1401 (1959).
5. Goldfine, H., and K. Bloch, *J. Biol. Chem.,* **236,** 2596 (1961).
6. Kaneshiro, T., and A. G. Marr, *J. Biol. Chem.,* **236,** 2615 (1961).
7. Hofmann, K., R. A. Lucas, and S. M. Sax, *J. Biol. Chem.,* **195,** 473 (1952).
8. Hofmann, K., and S. M. Sax, *J. Biol. Chem.,* **205,** 55 (1953).
9. Lutton, E. S., W. F. Huber, A. J. Mabis, and C. B. Stewart, *J. Am. Chem. Soc.,* **73,** 5206 (1951).
10. Kaneshiro, T., and A. G. Marr, *J. Lipid Research,* **3,** 184 (1962).
11. Hofmann, K., and F. Tausig, *J. Biol. Chem.,* **213,** 415 (1955).
12. Bloch, K., P. Baronowsky, H. Goldfine, W. J. Lennarz, R. Light, A. T. Norris, and G. Scheuerbrandt, *Federation Proc.,* **20,** 921 (1961).
13. Scheuerbrandt, G., and K. Bloch, *J. Biol. Chem.,* **237,** 2064 (1962).
14. Lennarz, W. J., G. Scheuerbrandt, and K. Bloch, *J. Biol. Chem.,* **237,** 664 (1962).
15. Hofmann, K., D. B. Henis, and C. Panos, *J. Biol. Chem.,* **228,** 349 (1957).
16. Kitay, E., and E. E. Snell, *J. Bact.,* **60,** 49 (1950).
17. Hofmann, K., W. M. O'Leary, C. W. Yoho, and T. Y. Liu, *J. Biol. Chem.,* **234,** 1672 (1959).
18. Hofmann, K., G. J. Marco, and G. A. Jeffrey, *J. Am. Chem. Soc.,* **80,** 5717 (1958).
19. Lemieux, R. U., and E. von Rudloff, *Can. J. Chem.,* **33,** 1701 (1955).
20. Klenk, E., and W. Bongard, *Z. Physiol. Chem.,* **290,** 181 (1952).

21. Hofmann, K., and T. Y. Liu, *Biochim. Biophys. Acta,* **37,** 364 (1960).
22. Liu, T. Y., and K. Hofmann, *Biochemistry,* **1,** 189 (1962).
23. O'Leary, W. M., *J. Bact.,* **77,** 367 (1959).
24. O'Leary, W. M., *J. Bact.,* **78,** 709 (1959).
25. Innes Chalk, K. J., and E. Kodicek, *Biochim. Biophys. Acta,* **50,** 579 (1961).
26. Danielsson, H., and K. Bloch, *J. Am. Chem. Soc.,* **79,** 500 (1957).
27. Alexander, G. J., and E. Schwenk, *J. Am. Chem. Soc.,* **79,** 4554 (1957).

BIOSYNTHESIS OF MONOUNSATURATED FATTY ACIDS BY MICROORGANISMS

1. GROWTH STUDIES

Since *cis*-vaccenic and lactobacillic acids are important constituents of the lipids of many microorganisms, and since these two acids are closely linked metabolically, we explored the biosynthetic routes to *cis*-vaccenic acid. As a point of departure, it was assumed (1, 2) that the biosynthesis of unsaturated fatty acids either may take place through desaturation of saturated long-chain fatty acids or may involve elongation of the carbon chain of an already unsaturated (or potentially unsaturated) precursor.

Suspensions of *L. arabinosus, L. casei,* and *L. delbrueckii* show no dehydrogenase activity toward stearic, palmitic, lauric, and myristic acids under a variety of experimental conditions (2). Since it was possible that the fatty acids are incapable of entering the cell, a series of experiments were conducted with ruptured cell preparations with similarly negative results. These observations in conjunction with the failure of saturated fatty acids to exert the typical sparing action of unsaturated fatty acids on the biotin requirements of various lactic acid organisms (Chapter 1, section 6) eliminated direct desaturation of long-chain saturated fatty acids as the pathway to unsaturated fatty acids. As it appeared more likely that the organisms introduce the unsaturation into a smaller molecule, which would then undergo elongation of its carbon chain through successive 2-carbon additions, we synthesized three unsaturated fatty acids of the general structure shown on Fig. 3.1 (where n represents 1, 3, and 5) and tested their ability to support growth of *L. arabinosus*, *L. casei*, and *L. delbrueckii* in presence of suboptimal amounts of biotin. Starting with *cis*-vaccenic acid ($n = 9$) and including palmitoleic acid ($n = 7$) a homologous series of five unsaturated acids differ-

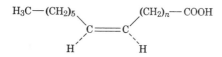

n	Acid
9	*cis*–vaccenic
7	palmitoleic
5	*cis*–7, 8–tetradecenoic
3	*cis*–5, 6–dodecenoic
1	*cis*–3, 4–decenoic

Fig. 3.1. Chemical structure of homologous series of unsaturated fatty acids.

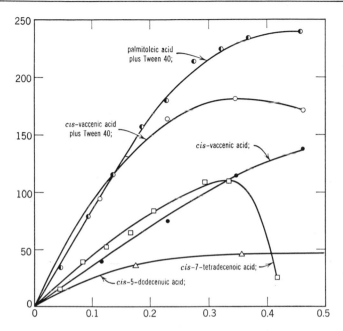

Fig. 3.2. Fatty acid growth curves for *L. arabinosus*. Abscissa, μmoles of fatty acid per tube. Ordinate, Klett readings.

ing from one another by successive 2-carbon shortening of the chain was available for study. The position of the double bond with respect to the methyl group was kept constant in this series of acids.

The ability of the organisms studied to utilize unsaturated *cis* acids possessing carbon chains shorter than *cis*-vaccenic acid (Figs. 3.2, 3.3, and 3.4) lends support to the hypothesis that unsaturated fatty acid biosynthesis may involve elongation of the carbon chain of a shorter chain unsaturated precursor. However, the short-chain acids may substitute

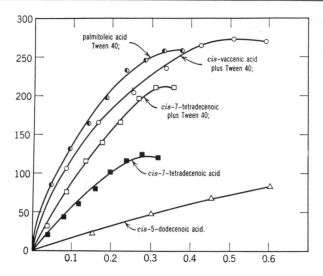

Fig. 3.3. Fatty acid growth curves for *L. casei*. Abscissa, μmoles of fatty acid per tube. Ordinate, Klett readings.

functionally for *cis*-vaccenic acid without undergoing chain elongation. *Cis*-vaccenic and palmitoleic acids exhibit approximately equal growth-promoting activity in all three organisms. The *cis*-7-tetradecenoic acid is somewhat less effective than the C_{16} and C_{18} acids. The *cis*-5-dodecenoic acid exhibits a low order of activity, and the *cis*-3-decenoic acid is inactive. In view of Wakil's demonstration of the role of biotin in saturated fatty acid biosynthesis (3), it is of interest to note that *cis*-7-tetradecenoic and *cis*-5-dodecenoic acids lose their ability to support growth for *L. arabinosus* when the bacteria used to inoculate the assay tubes are subjected to extensive washing with 0.85% sodium chloride. Biotin in amounts which failed to stimulate growth in absence of the fatty acids (0.05 mμg./tube) restored the growth-promoting potency of the fatty acids. This phenomenon was not observed with the other organisms, but more reliable growth curves were obtained when the media were fortified with 0.01 mμg. of biotin.

The growth-promoting activity of *cis*-vaccenic, palmitoleic, and *cis*-7,8-tetradecenoic acid for *L. casei* and *L. delbrueckii* is markedly increased by addition of Tween 40 to the culture medium. With *L. arabinosus*, the Tween 40 increased the stimulatory effects of *cis*-vaccenic and palmitoleic acids but suppressed the growth effect of *cis*-7-tetradecenoic acid.

The part played by the Tween is obscure but appears to

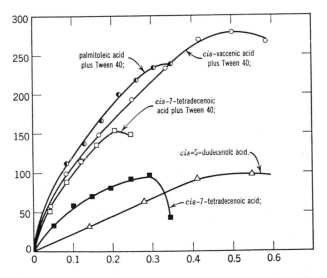

Fig. 3.4. Fatty acid growth curves for *L. delbrueckii*. Abscissa, μmoles of fatty acid per tube. Ordinate, Klett readings.

be more complex than to serve merely as a source of saturated fatty acids. Lactobacilli fail to grow on media low in biotin which are supplemented with unsaturated fatty acids and contain a saturated fatty acid in place of the Tween.

Cis-3,4-methylenedecanoic acid, the cyclopropane analog of *cis*-3-decenoic acid fails to promote growth of the organisms. The synthetic precursor acetylenic acids of the unsaturated acids, i.e., 3-decynoic, 5-dodecynoic, 7-tetradecynoic and 11-octadecynoic acids also lack growth promoting ability.

2. STUDIES WITH LABELED COMPOUNDS

That long-chain saturated fatty acids are incorporated into the lipids of *L. planarum* and *C. butyricum* is evident from the results which are summarized in Table 3.1. Stearic acid labeled with C^{14} is incorporated into the bacterial lipids, but the label is located almost exclusively in the saturated acid fraction. Labeling of the unsaturated fatty acids is insignificant.

TABLE 3.1

Lack of Desaturation of Stearate in Anaerobic Bacteria

	L. planarum c.p.m. $\times 10^{-3}$	*C. butyricum* c.p.m. $\times 10^{-3}$
C^{14} stearate added	1700	2000
C^{14} incorporated	720	500
Total saturated acids	700	490
Total unsaturated acids	<20	20

Adapted from Bloch et al., *Federation Proceedings*, **20,** 921 (1961).

TABLE 3.2

Incorporation of Saturated Acids into Long-Chain (C_{16} + C_{18}) Acids of *C. butyricum*

C^{14} Acid Added to Growth Medium *	Percent of Incorporated C^{14} in Saturated Acids	Percent of Incorporated C^{14} in Unsaturated Acids
C_2	60	40
C_8	75	25
C_{10}	80	20
C_{12}	96	4
C_{14}	96	4
C_{16}	97	3
C_{18}	99	1

* All the acids were labeled in the carboxyl group.
Adapted from Bloch et al., *Federation Proceedings*, **20,** 921 (1961).

These experiments which corroborate previous findings (1, 2) show clearly that permeability factors are not the reason for the inability of saturated fatty acids to substitute for unsaturated fatty acids as promoters of bacterial growth in biotin deficient media. They demonstrate in addition that *L. planarum* and *C. butyricum,* just as *L. arabinosus, L. casei,* and *L. delbrueckii,* cannot bring about desaturation of long-chain fatty acids.

Of particular significance is the observation (Table 3.2) that in contrast to saturated fatty acids containing 12, 14, 16, and 18 carbon atoms, octanoate-1-C^{14} and decanoate-1-C^{14} are incorporated into both the saturated and the monounsaturated fatty acids of *C. butyricum* (4, 5). As can be expected, acetate also serves as a precursor of both types of fatty acids. The distribution of radioactivity in the hexadecenoic and octadecenoic acids provides the experimental basis for a plausible mechanism of anaerobic unsaturated fatty acid biosynthesis (6).

Of importance for appreciation of this mechanism is the fact that *C. butyricum* contains two pairs of homologous unsaturated fatty acids, namely, 7,8-hexadecenoic-oleic and 9,10-hexadecenoic-*cis*-vaccenic acids. The acids in each pair differ from each other by one "C_2" unit at the carboxyl end but the distance between the methyl group and double bond is identical, i.e., seven methylene groups in the oleic and five methylene groups in the *cis*-vaccenic pair of acids.

The hexadecenoic and octadecenoic acid fractions from the octanoate and decanoate grown organisms, respectively, were oxidized by the Lemieux procedure (7) and the ensuing dicarboxylic acids were separated by gas chromatography as the methyl esters. With octanoate-1-C^{14} as the precursor, only the C_9 dicarboxylic acid from the hexadecanoate and the C_{11} dicarboxylic acid from the octadecanoate are radioactive. In experiments with decanoate-1-C^{14} the label is located predominantly in the C_7 dicarboxylic acid from the hexadecenoate fraction and the C_9 dicarboxylic acid from the octadecenoic acids. These results show that the short-chain acids are indeed converted into the long-chain unsaturated acids by multiple addition of "C_2" units as predicted from our growth studies (2) and that direct double-bond interconversions do not occur. Based on the distribution of label in the unsaturated fatty acids, Scheuerbrandt et al. (6) suggested a scheme (Fig. 3.5) for the biosynthesis of unsaturated fatty acids in anaerobes, which appears to fit presently available experimental evidence.

Octanoate (upper left) is postulated to undergo two different types of reaction with a "C_2" unit to form either decanoate or via a hypothetical 3-hydroxydecanoic acid 3,4-decenoic acid. This latter acid, through multiple addi-

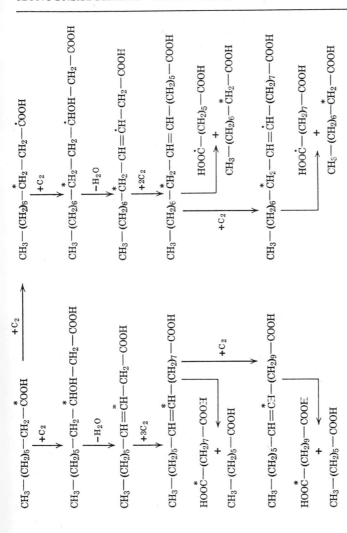

Fig. 3.5. Plausible route for anaerobic unsaturated fatty acid biosynthesis as postulated by Scheuerbrandt et al. (5).

tions of "C_2" units, is converted into palmitoleic acid and finally cis-vaccenic acid.

Decanoate (upper right) may undergo the same types of chain elongation as octanoate with formation of 3,4-dodecenoic acid via the hypothetical 3-hydroxydodecanoate. Chain elongation of 3,4-dodecenoic acid by subsequent "C_2" additions brings about formation of oleic acid via 7,8-hexadecenoic acid. Concurrently, both octanoate and decanoate may undergo chain elongation with formation of palmitic and stearic acids. This biosynthetic route to monounsaturated fatty acids differs markedly from that present in yeast *M. phlei* and mammalian liver which involves dehydrogenation of palmitic or stearic acids via reactions requiring oxygen and TPNH (4).

3. METABOLISM OF MONOUNSATURATED FATTY ACIDS IN BACTERIA

Lactobacilli cannot synthesize saturated or unsaturated fatty acids in absence of biotin, but cells grown on a supplement of oleic or cis-vaccenic acid contain large proportions of saturated fatty acids, mainly palmitic acid. Since the media employed are supplemented with Tween 40 (sorbitan monopalmitate) the Tween may have provided the source for the palmitic acid. As has been mentioned (Chapter 2, section 3 and Chapter 3, section 1), the Tween is essential for growth of many organisms on biotin-low media supplemented with unsaturated or cyclopropane fatty acids.

Our own experiments (8) (Fig. 3.6) and those of our former collaborator O'Leary (9) with *L. arabinosus* cultured on cis-vaccinate-l-C^{14} eliminate saturation of monounsaturated fatty acids as a route to saturated fatty acids in this

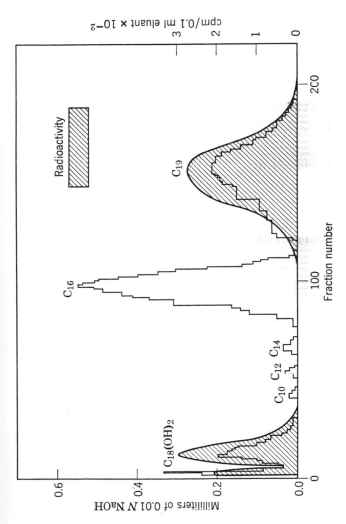

Fig. 3.6. Distribution of radioactivity in fatty acids from *L. arabinosus* cells grown on *cis*-vaccenic acid-1-C14.

organism.   The results of Bloch et al. (4) (Table 3.3) with oleic acid grown *L. planarum* and *M. phlei* are in excellent agreement with our own findings.   Thus, one must conclude that these organisms are unable to convert unsaturated into saturated fatty acids.   Their inability to effect the opposite reaction, i.e., desaturation of long-chain saturated fatty acids has been discussed.

It appears that the major metabolic role of monounsaturated fatty acids in the bacteria is that of a precursor for the biosynthesis of cyclopropane or methyl branched fatty acids.   The first clue in support of this now well-established fact was our observation (10) that *L. delbrueckii,* grown on biotin low media in presence of lactobacillic acid, fails to synthesize unsaturated fatty acids.   These acids are present in high proportions in the lipids of biotin grown cells.   We confirmed these observations with *L. arabinosus* and *L. casei* (2).   The high degree of labeling of the cyclopropane acid fraction in *L. planarum* and of the 10-methylstearic acid fraction in *M. phlei,* when the organisms are cultured on oleic acid-1-C^{14} (Table 3.3), shows that "methylation"

TABLE 3.3

Transformation of 1-C^{14} Oleic Acid by Microorganisms

	L. planarum c.p.m. $\times 10^{-3}$	*M. phlei* c.p.m. $\times 10^{-6}$
C^{14} Oleate added	760	1350
Total fatty acids	220	338
Palmitic acid	1	20
Stearic acid	2	2
C^{19} Cyclopropane acid	75	
10-Methylstearic acid		200

Adapted from Bloch et al., *Federation Proceedings*, **20,** 921 (1961).

is a major metabolic fate of the unsaturated fatty acids. In organisms such as *C. butyricum* and *E. coli,* which contain both C_{16} and C_{18} unsaturated fatty acids, "methylation" takes place with formation of a mixture of C_{17} and C_{19} cyclopropane fatty acids (see Chapter 2, section 5).

The chemical nature of the cyclopropane fatty acids, which arise when the microorganisms are cultured on oleic rather than on *cis*-vaccenic acid, remains to be established—but two possibilities exist for oleic acid metabolism. Either the double bond undergoes isomerization with formation of *cis*-vaccenic acid, which in turn is metabolized to lactobacillic acid, or the bacteria have the ability to "methylate" oleic acid with formation of one of the optical isomers of dihydrosterculic acid. O'Leary (9) suggested that *L. arabinosus* brings about isomerization of added oleic acid with formation of *cis*-vaccenic plus lactobacillic acids, but his experimental evidence in support of this unlikely course is not convincing. We find (10) that oleic acid grown *L. delbrueckii* produce a liquid saturated fatty acid fraction which exhibits 1.6 times the growth promoting activity of pure lactobacillic acid in *L. delbrueckii* assays. Since dihydrosterculic acid, which contains the methylene bridge in the 9,10-position, is 1.4 times as active in the same assay as lactobacillic acid with the 11,12-methylene bridge, we concluded (10) "that oleic acid stimulates *L. delbrueckii* to produce a 'saturated' fatty acid exhibiting higher microbiological activity than that of lactobacillic acid."

Scheuerbrandt et al. (6) using *C. butyricum* demonstrated that this organism does not interconvert unsaturated fatty acids containing 5 methylene groups between the methyl terminus and the double bond into fatty acids having 7 methylene groups in that location. Thus, the available evidence suggests that the organisms are capable of bringing about "methylation" of double bonds in long-chain fatty acids with double-bond locations five and seven methylene groups removed from the methyl end with formation of the corresponding cyclopropane fatty acids. However, isolation and careful chemical characterization of the "methylation product" of oleic acid must be carried out in order to establish this point unequivocally.

Mention was made in Chapter 1, section 6, of the experiments of Cheng et al. (11) who showed that a number of position isomeric octadecanoic acids possessing both *cis* and *trans* double bonds have the ability to stimulate growth of *L. arabinosus* on suboptimal amounts of biotin. The mode of action of such acids is at present obscure. The possibility exists that they may be converted into the corresponding position isomeric *cis* or *trans* cyclopropane acids and that these may have the ability to serve as metabolic substitutes for lactobacillic acid. However, it seems unlikely that a family of compounds of such widely differing structure and belonging to different stereochemical series should be capable of performing the same or similar functions in microbial metabolism. Similar arguments may be raised concerning the mode of action of the polyunsaturated fatty acids (linoleic, linolenic, and arachidonic), which are also capable of promoting growth of lactic acid organisms on biotin deficient media. Are these polyunsaturated acids undergoing "methylation" with formation of acids containing more than one cyclopropane ring?

Studies on the metabolic fate of these various acids and a better understanding of the role of the cyclopropane fatty acids in microbial metabolism should aid in clarification of these questions.

REFERENCES

1. O'Leary, W. M., and K. Hofmann, *Federation Proc.,* **16,** 228 (1957).
2. Hofmann, K., W. M. O'Leary, C. W. Yoho, and T. Y. Liu, *J. Biol. Chem.,* **234,** 1672 (1959).
3. Wakil, S. J., E. B. Titchener, and D. M. Gibson, *Biochim. Biophys. Acta,* **29,** 225 (1958).
4. Bloch, K., P. E. Baronowsky, H. Goldfine, W. J. Lennarz, R. Light, A. T. Norris, and G. Scheuerbrandt, *Federation Proc.,* **20,** 921 (1961).
5. Goldfine, H., and K. Bloch, *J. Biol. Chem.,* **236,** 2596 (1961).
6. Scheuerbrandt, G., H. Goldfine, P. E. Baronowsky, and K. Bloch, *J. Biol. Chem.,* **236,** PC70 (1961).
7. Lemieux, R. U., and E. von Rudloff, *Can. J. Chem.,* **33,** 1701 (1955).
8. Liu, T. Y., and K. Hofmann, *Biochemistry,* **1,** 189 (1962).
9. O'Leary, W. M., *J. Bact.,* **77,** 367 (1959).
10. Hofmann, K., D. B. Henis, and C. Panos, *J. Biol. Chem.,* **228,** 349 (1957).
11. Cheng, A. L. S., S. M. Greenberg, H. J. Deuel, Jr., and D. Melnick, *J. Biol. Chem.,* **192,** 611 (1951).

INDEX